ONE OF THE TWELVE...

"HE WILL SHOW YOU A LARGE ROOM UPSTAIRS, ALL FURNISHED...

"MAKE PREPARATIONS THERE."

PART II

THE SIXTH HOUR...

AND THEIR SHOUTS PREVAILED.

IT WAS NOW ABOUT NOON, AND DARKNESS CAME OVER THE WHOLE LAND UNTIL THREE IN THE AFTERNOON,

FOR THE SUN STOPPED SHINING.

AND THE CURTAIN OF THE TEMPLE...

WAS TORN IN TWO.

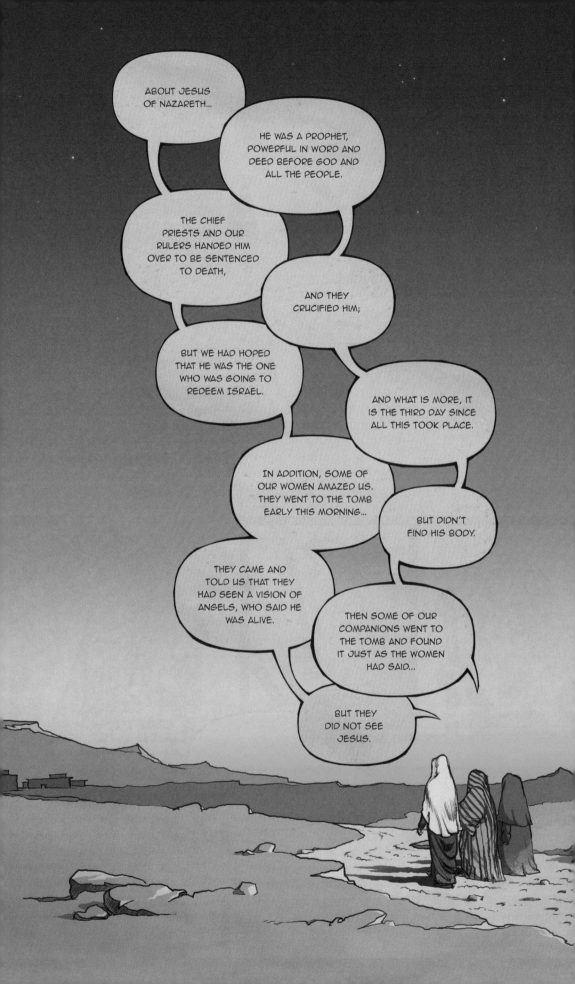